THE INSATIABLE WORDS

WHERE WORDS HAVE NO CURBS

M. A. KHAN

ISBN 979-888546442-0

Contents

Acknowledgements

I am just a young writer. But not one with just a pen in my hands, I have dreams, imagination and ideas all around my head. In this, my first publication. I have tried my best to write down a short collection of all my works of past one year. And over the course of time I'll definitely learn new things from experiences like this and will be looking forward to writing more such works. I am entirely thankful to my parents for supporting me in my interests in writing. Also this collection would have been incomplete without the help of my brother, I thank him for encouraging me in my different stages of life and making me hold onto the writing, paving paths to the future of my writings.

Poems

1. The bird who didn't fly

Birds often will to fly,
But sat there one without a try.
It was a raven sitting alight,
As my pen recalls the sight.
There were birds of many kinds,
Robins and starlings flying aligned.
But all of them couldn't catch the eye,
For a raven there didn't fly.
The silent statue stated there,
Held in me questions here.
Isn't the sky, your kingdom great?
Why don't you fly? With all the haste!
I was then backed by surprise,
For yes it did answer, from its eyes!
Mind filled of regrets and heart bounded by fear,
Thoughts of griefs lacking any cheer.
Chained by its thoughts it couldn't fly,
There it sat just thinking by.
But, it was only resting there
As once as for all, it had to fly.
And I swear so do I.
Just then with a flap of wide black wings,
Dived the raven with all its limbs.

Far away it flew, leaving me behind
With all the questions struck in my mind.
For I wished to be the raven,
The one who fled.
But I was the bird,
Who didn't fly.

2. So close, yet so far

Into the winds of early winter,
My eyes caught a sight, rest all looked fainter.
Within the darkness I saw some light,
The moon and star, held close so tight.
The star concealed to farthest heights,
The moon had its own, festival of lights!
To the west laid the moon afar,
Helding host to the evening star.
It did it's best to illude the eyes,
So close they looked, were held so far.
Into the silence my thoughts went harsh,
They reminded me of souls, apart!
For humans claim to held one's near,
Yet this soul, thrives in fear.
Their jaws utter the best of rhymes,
Yet their actions beats all the crimes.
Their vows render all bounds,
With time these vows are truly unfound.
They ask out why, the face stays pale,
Yet in need hide Adam's ale.
They tend to be the closest shrine,
Where we stay most vulnerably, fine!
Indeed they illude the hearts so strong,

The eyes veiled, and minds so wronged.
But In the end, my thoughts went calm!
Into solitude they did no harm.
For humans are the moon and star,
So close he made them, yet so far

3. I wanted, but nothing did

I wanted to fly, but I had no broomstick.
I wanted to swim deep under water
But I had no gillyweed.
I wanted to be invisible,
But I had no cloak.
I wanted to share all my secrets, but I had no friends.
I wanted a home,
But I had no Hogwarts.
I wanted to live,
But I had no magic.
I wanted to love,
But I had no heart'.
I wanted to die,
But I already did. I wanted... but nothing did.

4. The Rooftop

Winds rushed through me from every direction.
I stood alone on the roof top without an intention
Birds flew past me without hesitation
I stood still without an impression
Thoughts of someone arouse without an invitation
Sorrow along the grievance of the world emerged in the occasion
I closed my eyes lacking any objection
The memories faded away as a reflection
These memories stood deep inside me without any condition
And, I won't part from it till my extinction
Then, I felt the winds pushing me with its best aggression
I opened my eyes and arouse a situation.
Where I stood on the rooftop,
Alone, - Without an intention.

5. Changes

Every day I wake up, I arise with a change,
Every day that passes by,
Gives me a change,
Every moment I live
I change, this change should happen or not?
I don't know.
Is it good or bad?
I don't know.
Is it harmful for me?
I don't know.
The only thing I know is,
This change makes me sick,
Sick on myself.
I have begun doing things I didn't,
And I left doing things I did.
Where this will lead me? I don't know.
What should I do?
I don't know.
I have no power left to fight myself.
So I don't question myself.
This is a change,
What to do?
I don't know.

6. Our-Memories

A year comes and goes, like the melting of snow.
Seasons visit us and leave, by the change of wind.
A child born grows, by the aging of leaves.
Everything around us changes, but the only thing that remains untouched
Are our MEMORIES.
The ones that make us smile, and mourn.
The ones that bring us near, and apart.
The ones that remind us to live, and love.
The ones that stay inside of us now, And forever.
Our-Memories

Quotations

A time will surely come when you feel

everything in life is falling apart

Don't grab the things that make you happy,

grab the things that make you live.

-

What will I do by shining in the day?

If there's a desire to shine, 'll shine in the darkness.

-

Looking for me?

-look to the farthest horizon.

Finding the farthest horizon?

-look at me.

-

The world is beautiful my dear,

It's my eyes who have turned dark.

-

For long this soul has been in longing.

Either keep it alive, or bury it deep.

-

Words create my unspoken dream.

-

The past stays dark,

the future still hidden,

and the present goes unseen.

-

Thoughts change every night,

dreams stay with you for eternity

-

My time of leisure is conceived

of the greatest truth of life. Death!

-

The deepest of my thoughts

ends up being the darkest.

-

Some moments cannot be classified

as good or bad, happy or sad.

And that's life.

-

When there's darkness within,

the world outside seems no longer beautiful.

-

In the idle run of life,

somewhere I'm lost between

the obligatory and the needful

-

We don't die when our heart stops beating,

we die when it stops feeling.

-

Lucky are those who have

someone's shoulder to cry

and wipe their tears on.

Strong are those who cry without tears,

-

A thousand reasons to hide the face,

not a single face to know one reason.

-

There were times I wished to sit

in a corner of the world

and cry wholeheartedly,

but the world betrayed me

for having no corners.

-

The people who wander alone

are not the saddest,

but who do not expect anything

from this mean world.

-

After watching the fate of a rose,

very few like it the same way.

-

On the quest to find a tired soul,

in complete darkness.

All you need is a little light.

-

Love is destructive if taken deeply,

Venom is taken lightly,

and a blessing if left untouched.

-

Weary were my eyes

looking for solitude

in this happy world.

Rejoiced have they been,

since I found it in myself.

-

I don't sleep nowadays

cause I can't dream.

I stay up in the dark,

and write them myself.

Then, chase them down

the day.

-

The silent mind

sleeps the best.

For this soul,

there's no rest.

-

Stop looking at life from

the mirror of expectations.

Look it through the reality of the soul.

-

Learn to stand alone today,

to stand apart tomorrow.

-

Thoughts

Night Sky

Extraordinary beauty thrives

beyond the veil of darkness,

unseen to the human eye.

Long has this darkness feared man on earth,

In silence it hides beauty beyond our imagination.

-

These nights never changed.

All that did, was a silent dweller

who dreamed.

-

Winter's Evening

The calmness wins the

winter's evening.

Every breadth feels a

new beginning.

-

Discovering Destinations

Not all discoveries are made

by moving forward.

Sometimes all you need to

find your destination is,

A step backwards.

-

Pain builds you

The best of words ever said

are the ones said in pain.

For the reality is what has devastated

so many lives. Indeed happiness is

based on knowledge, the greater you know

about the reality, greater the pain you suffer.

-

Déjà Vu

Back to, The same place,

The same season,

The same roads,

The same reason.

Lost some people on the way,

And gained some at the bay.

In the end, here I stand again

where I stood once.

What have I gained?

-

Solitude

The ultimate fate of the soul is solitude,

into the darkness a never ending silence.

Others may define it as death.

-

Reality

We are all chasing a ton of desires.

Without having an ounce to plant them.

And that leaves us with nothing but

failure, regret and sorrow.

-

The Good Ones

Sometimes, In order to get a 'happy ending',

We neglect the rejoiceful moments.

In order to achieve a 'perfect future',

We overlook the better today.

In order to find 'the best one',

We disregard the good ones.

-

Life's Phases

There are two phases in life,

'Tough' and 'Easy'.

No matter in which phase we are,

Always remember; One day we're goanna go through

the other one.

-

Love's Lasting

If you ask me, ' How long will I love you?'

My answer will be 'I don't know.'

because I don't really know, which one is longer

'Always' or 'Forever'.

-

A Dead flower

Everyone left it,

In its darkest hour.

Now we complain,

For it smells sour.

We search for love,

Within its corpses.

Once it was also,

A bright flower.

-

In the Rain

Another day spent in vain

whispered my head while drenched in rain.

Standing there nothing I gained,

The thoughts finally numbed my brain.

I wish these raindrops washed all the pain.

-

Expectations

If the world was not bounded

by Expectations therein.

I would have lived my life,

with just heaps of paper and a pen.

-

A Petal over a Beloved

If I could lose a rose petal

for an increase in number of my beloveds.

I would lose my entire garden, and still

keep a petal near, just to call it mine.

-

Sorrow's Reality

All the sorrows we've ever heard.

Are the ones expressed.

Profound regret leaves the soul speechless,

True sorrow has no acquaintance.

-

The one's who really die

The ones who die without tasting the essence of

true love, are the ones actually dead.

Because true love makes you immortal.

Buried in the hearts of our beloveds.

-

Don't stress too much

What does it do?

For a soul to thrive in fear of the unseen.

When neither it benefits the world nor does

the world benefits from it.

Why does he has to exist?

When neither it is ready for the unseen,

nor is the unseen ready for it.

-

Thoughts upon Thoughts

By far, the most beautiful and

the most dangerous place to get lost is,

into the thoughts.

-

The Beginning Of A New Journey

The best of epilogue is what has led to this. Over the course of time, I have always appreciated and looked forward to the ends.

The end of something beautiful is necessary, for that is what makes us stronger, these ends keep the spirit of learning from experiences alive within us.

The end of something is the beginning of another. New ideas, thoughts and imagination can only thrive once you learn from your past experiences. And move forward to a new better start.

Till then I hope you read and relate to my works.

See you soon.

9 798885 464420

Printed by Libri Plureos GmbH in Hamburg, Germany